How to av

A small book about important things.
Published by Beehive, the agency alternative.

Published by Beehive.
3–5 Bateman Street,
London W1D 4AG
workingbeehive.co.uk

© Beehive 2019
Printed and bound in Great Britain
by Clays Ltd, Elcograf S.p.A.

ISBN 9781–5272–4899–1

With thanks to
Paul Belford for design.
paulbelford.com

How to avoid brand bullshit

What this book isn't about

This book isn't about preaching, there are no earth-shattering new theories, no eureka perspectives or clever musings on the future of this or that. We are not trying to, nor wish to be, gurus.

This book is about common sense and doing things well.

It's a simple distillation of on the job, coalface learning, from three guys who have the experience to share it.

It's a hands on, get stuff done perspective, designed to help focus on the stuff that needs focus. We hope it's helpful.

Worth a read?

The brand thing

You're in business, not in a gallery

A business is a repeatable process that makes money.

How is your brand going to help with that?

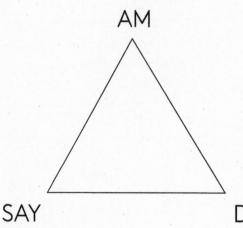

Brand story
competitive rationale

AM

SAY

External
communication

DO

Internal
operations/
behaviour

Be useful

Strategy is simply the choices you make: what you do and don't do.

It's the same for brands. The pyramids, boxes, visions purpose, missions etc can be useful, but it's what people get that matters and the choices you make in delivering that. Brands are actions not 'think pieces'.

What's the purpose of purpose?

It must be purposeful.

Often it's up it's own arse, meaningless. Here's one from a recent IPO prospectus for a rental office company: *'Our mission is to elevate the world's consciousness'.*

Be realistic.

If you have to have one, please make it relatable to your business and real people. Just work out how to make someone's life just a little bit better.

It's the category stupid

People choose category before brand.[*] If you don't know yours, or choose the wrong one, you're wasting everyone's time and your money.

Categories are often emotional as much as rational. Work at it, it's worth it.

*Thank you Byron Sharpe, 'How brands Grow.'

Chilled well-being

Yes this is a real one.

If your category doesn't make sense to ordinary folk, it's crap; no matter how smart you are.

Fix the fixable first

If people aren't buying, don't just rush at more brand stuff.

Ask:

— Does it cost too much?

— Does it work/not work?

— Does it work/not work for the right people?

— Is it too difficult to get/do/ be part of?

— Does it address a problem that's not much of a problem?

It's not all about you

Being distinctive and relevant
means leveraging the
right context around the brand,
category and life in general.

Choosing the right context is
a true, creative brand act.

Dog food is for dog owners

Make sure you really know who you want to talk to and why.

Obvious, but don't get lazy.

'I find it an interesting challenge to write for Mick. There's no point in giving him a song that's beyond his range or that he's not comfortable with.

What I really like to do is write a song where Mick goes:
    "Yer right I'm in"...'

'My job is to give him a riff that he leaps on and goes:
    "Right I know what to do with that"...'

— Keith Richards

Be humble

Insight means being insightful, duh!

About somebody.

People don't think straight, so work with their world-view; don't try to change the world.

Desire for gain
or avoidance of loss?

The name of the game is...

People identify with other people's hopes, problems and challenges. What are people really after?

Is it:

Small for many?

Big for a few?

Small multiple times?

Big multiple times?

Satisfaction is born of dissatisfaction

Often avoiding disaster is more important to people than achieving perfection.

So leveraging dissatisfaction, (expressed or unexpressed) is always worthwhile.

Brand questions worth asking:

1. What is the most distinctively competitive emotional category your business could/should be in?

2. Why will that matter emotionally and practically to your customers, especially the potential ones?

3. What group of people can become your initial group customers who will spread the word about the change/ re-start of your business?

4. What are customers dissatisfied with in relation to other choices (expressed or unexpressed)?

5. Why are they not well served, or not served at all, by the competition?

6. Why is your business the antidote/ answer to this; what problem do you solve a lot better than anyone else?

The communication thing

Don't say much

There's a lot of bollocks talked about storytelling.

Just make sure your story has:

— inspiration
— relatability
— surprise

What's the story?

Avoid the tendency to have a lot to say.

Two brand communication objectives
are enough. And try to sum up your brand
with just a few words, not sentences.

Two pairs of eyes

Distinctiveness and differentiation are the two communication lenses you need.

Distinctiveness is the reason to stand out—your own symbolic vocabulary.

Differentiation is the reason to believe — that makes you different to the competition.

Lead with distinctiveness, related to your differentiation.

Normal surprise

Don't be utterly original.

People like familiar, reassur

Aim for 20% new, 80% fan

Uber was positioned as 'a r
app' ... easy to understand
done in a new way.

Round pegs in square holes

Juxtapositions are a good way to
do the relevant unexpected and offer
familiar surprises ...

... bit like chess boxing.

Making sense isn't always sensible

If you don't have feeling, you have nothing.

If people feel nothing, they do nothing.

Let people join the dots

After many years making films
Steven Spielberg was asked what he
had learnt about making movies.

'Put less on the film', he replied. 'People
enjoy the reward of joining the dots'.

So make that happen.

Personalisation isn't personal

Personalisation can waste a lot of time, money and hassle.

The ability to communicate in a personal way is a better way to do it, and it's more personal.

Communication technology is not communication

People change a lot more slowly than the tech does. Focus on the people more than the technology.

Be anti-social

Social media is not a replacement for share of voice.

Reach is more impactful than buzz.

Spend wisely

Roughly 60% of your money is typically optimal for your longer-term brand building, 40% on shorter-term sales/activation.*

Choose your media appropriate for each job. The data is there to support this.

*Thank you Les Binet, Peter Field and the IPA.
Please read their stuff, it's so good.

Get stuck in a rut

Being consistent pays off.

Get a good creative brand idea
and stick with it.

Change the expression by
all means, but keep the idea
consistent.

COLUMBO

WHAT: well thought out crime is always discovered
WHO: by the super smart thinking detective
HOW: being cleverer and more forensic than
the criminals
CUSTOMER BENEFIT: ensuring crime doesn't pay
and keeping Americans safer

DIRTY HARRY

WHAT: perfect justice is restored
WHO: by the enforcer of the law
HOW: being more violent than the criminals
CUSTOMER BENEFIT: helping vulnerable Americans
to stay safe

Know thyself

Know how to define your creative idea and make sure your creative partners can do likewise.

If they can't, you don't have an idea.

Communication keys:

1. Keep communication objectives manageable and sum up your brand in just a few words.

2. Ensure you have inspiration, relatability and surprise.

3. Distinctiveness and differentiation: you need both.

4. Don't be utterly original: follow the 80/20 rule.

5. Juxtapositions work to engender creativity.

6. You must create feeling and a sense of the personal.

7. Let people join the dots, don't spell out everything.

8. Define your idea before buying anything.

9. If possible, stick with a good idea that delivers all of the above.

The creative thing

How to help judge ideas.

Some really useful things
for you and your creatives
to talk about.

Your job when working with creatives

Zzzzzzzzzzzz. Avoid this at all costs.

Does the idea have genuine impact?

Have the courage to kill the
baby before it gets too ugly*

*Thank you John Hegarty.

JUST WHEN YOU THINK IT CAN'T GET ANY WORSE...

Let's not forget we are in the business of persuasion.

If the idea doesn't persuade you, it probably won't persuade anyone else.

But just how do you persuade people?

Logic will get you so far, but the best kind of persuasion is inspiration.

Just ask Barack Obama.

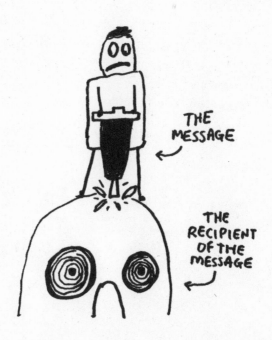

THE MESSAGE

THE RECIPIENT OF THE MESSAGE

Does the idea have impactful relevance?

Does the idea grab attention?
If it doesn't, everything else will
be irrelevant.

While you're at it, check to
see if it says something relevant.

Most ideas don't ...

... grabbing attention and saying something relevant are crucial ingredients to your idea.

If you get these two things right, the idea will stick in the consumer's minds and you may well have a hit on your hands.

Does it have an impactful idea at its core?

Great scripts need an idea.

It's helpful that the idea is summarised at the top of the script.

Then you'll be able to judge whether the script is doing the idea justice.

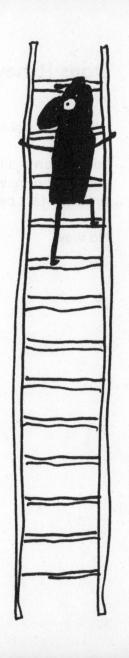

Does it have boldness?

Is the idea bold?

You've come a long way with your brand, now is not the time to start being ordinary.

No way.

Does the idea make you feel anything?

Always trust your gut instincts.
They rarely let you down.

If you're ambivalent about an idea, don't waste your time on it.

Move on quickly to the next one.

Creativity is a construction of chaotic thoughts and feelings that somehow combine to make magic.

The more functional an idea is, the less likely it is that consumers will engage with it.

Always look for the magic because magic is what people want to see.

Hollywood has taught us that storytelling is visual as well as verbal.

When reading a script, remember it's hard to engage an audience with wall-to-wall words.

It's an ad, not a lecture.

The best scripts are sparse and pared down to allow the visuals to speak as well as the dialogue.

Film is a visual medium, the more words there are, the less it will communicate.

Ideas that touch people are more powerful, so ideas with emotion will linger longer in the consumer's mind and make people feel something about your brand.

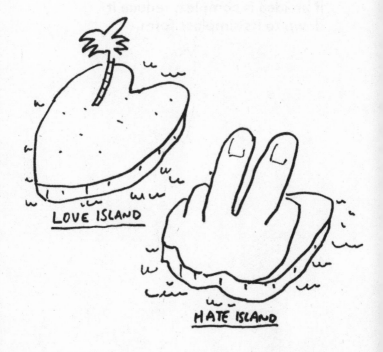

LOVE ISLAND

HATE ISLAND

Can it convince simply?

Is the idea simple?

Could you explain it to an alien?

Advertising is about the art of reduction.

If an idea is complex, reduce it down to its simplest form.

Who is it for, is it somebody or anyone?

Know your audience. Know exactly who you are talking to.

Be specific. Think of an individual.

This way you'll know if the tone of voice is right.

When judging an idea, it's good to remember that nobody will actually care about it unless there's a reason to give a toss.

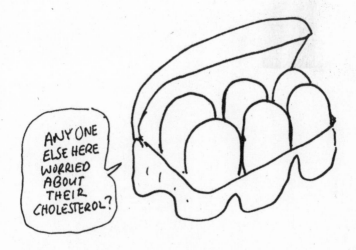

Is it rooted in anything about the people you want to attract?

All great ideas start life with a great insight. Check the idea has one.

If it has, make sure it's singing loud and proud. A killer insight is the springboard to originality.

It changes the game and kills off the competition.

ONE SHOE IS NOT ENOUGH.

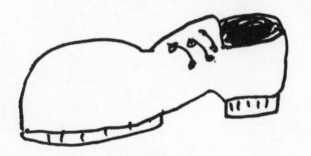

Is it rooted in anything about your brand?

The truth is: ideas need truth to work.

Truth is the fundamental building block of any idea. It's what gives an idea its integrity.

Without integrity, you are nowhere.

Does it have a personality that works for your brand?

Humour is the most difficult form of script to judge. Tread carefully.

Remember, funny scripts on paper rarely translate into funny films.

Don't look for written gags, but work out if the idea is intrinsically funny.

If it is, humour will flow freely from it.

Great ideas love irreverence. Let's face it, we all love irreverence. It makes people sit up and reassess.

It asks questions. It helps make new concepts understandable. It can make an ordinary idea exceptional.

If you want to break a mould, try a dollop of irreverence.

THE FLATULENT NUN.

Wit often goes hand in hand with irreverence.

Wit is smart humour. If you want a smart brand, choose wit.

BATTLE OF WITS.

Does the idea have charm? Charm is often the missing ingredient and the reason most communications are ignored.

The idea doesn't have to be littered with meerkats to make it charming.

Charm comes in all shapes and sizes. Even Genghis Khan had a certain charm. Find your own charm.

Is there love in the work for your brand

Whether it's you and your brand or a writer creating an idea for your brand, caring about what you do is the defining factor between success and failure.

If somebody loves what they do, you'll see it shining through. Look for the love.

The creative thing:

1. Does the idea have genuine impact?

2. Does it make you feel anything?

3. Can it convince simply?

4. Is it for somebody?

5. Is it simple to grasp?

6. Is it rooted in anything about the people you want to attract?

7. Is it truthful and ownable?

8. Does it have a personality which works for your brand?

The production thing

How to work with Producers
and Directors.

Some insightful questions
about making your ideas.

There are no problems

What's the golden rule about production? It should never, ever be a problem. It's the Producer's job to make it so, no exceptions.

On the pitch before the game starts

How do you know you're working with a great Producer?

Two things: expectation and anticipation. Meaning do they surround themselves with really good experts and do they spot problems *before* they could happen and tell you about them?

Two deadly sins

So what do you usually have to watch out for?

Timelines and money. These are the things that trip people up — not enough of either agreed up-front. Get them agreed and understood before you do anything else.

Open all frequencies

What does a Producer need from clients more than anything else?

Fast, honest feedback and decisions made decisively. So clients need to be shown stuff ASAP without lots of agency interference. Get as much squared away as far in advance as possible, especially cast and locations, if using them.

Work with the species

What do you need to know about Directors? Well, they all have ego, the desire for a sense of 'look at me', a certain showing off, even if they're hiding it. You need that to be a Director, so work with it.

Talent scout

What does a Producer do in relation to
the Director?

The job is to pick the right one, matching
up the right Director to each script or
shoot. Some are better all rounders, some
are specialists. You need to know which.
And try and pick Directors who will
get on with the creative teams, that helps.

Get involved

Should clients talk to Directors?

Keeping clients away from Directors is a big mistake. There needs to be a direct relationship to create trust, speed, clarity, precision and getting stuff done on time.

Clients should ask if they don't understand a technique and make time to be involved.

On the money

What are you expecting Directors
to deliver?

Firstly when you talk to them
you can clearly see that they are
going to add something extra;
a little bit of magic to the script.
Secondly you need to feel that
they are capable of being able to
deliver on their promises.

Creative promises

What's the role of the Creatives with the Director?

They may not have a clue how to do it but they should have a sense of how it should be. Get them to explain it to you and the Director.

Afterwards

What is good post-production?

Whatever it is, it should look real.
If it doesn't you have a problem.
It's not about the clever machinery,
but the individuals. Ask about
the individuals, not the techniques.

A magic brush up

Can post-production do miracles?

In my experience anything can
be done in post and all things can
be fixed, at a price.

Soon and later

When does post-production
get involved?

If it's complicated they should be
around early in the process.
Let them have a supervisor on
the shoot.

The production thing:

1. Producers solve problems before there are problems. Make sure yours is good at doing that.

2. Get clear on timelines and budgets before you do anything else. It avoids issues later.

3. As the client, provide fast, honest feedback and be decisive.

4. Use your Producer to find the right Director/Photographer.